People in My Community

Doctor

by Jacqueline Laks Gorman
Photographs by Gregg Andersen

Reading consultant: Susan Nations, M.Ed., author/literacy coach/consultant

WEEKLY WR READER®
EARLY LEARNING LIBRARY

Please visit our web site at: **www.earlyliteracy.cc**
For a free color catalog describing Weekly Reader® Early Learning Library's
list of high-quality books, call 1-877-445-5824 (USA) or 1-800-387-3178 (Canada).
Weekly Reader® Early Learning Library's fax: (414) 336-0164.

Library of Congress Cataloging-in-Publication Data

Gorman, Jacqueline Laks, 1955-
     Doctor / by Jacqueline Laks Gorman.
          p. cm. — (People in my community)
     Summary: Provides an easy-to-read explanation of what a doctor does.
     Includes bibliographical references and index.
     ISBN 0-8368-3294-9 (lib. bdg.)
     ISBN 0-8368-3301-5 (softcover)
     1. Medicine—Juvenile literature.   2. Physicians—Juvenile literature.
     [1. Physicians.   2. Occupations.]   I. Title.
     R690.G66   2002
     610.69'52—dc21   2002023886

This edition first published in 2002 by
Weekly Reader® Early Learning Library
330 West Olive Street, Suite 100
Milwaukee, WI 53212 USA

Copyright © 2002 by Weekly Reader® Early Learning Library

Art direction and page layout: Tammy Gruenewald
Photographer: Gregg Andersen
Editorial assistant: Diane Laska-Swanke
Production: Susan Ashley

Printed in the United States of America

1 2 3 4 5 6 7 8 9 06 05 04 03 02

Note to Educators and Parents

Reading is such an exciting adventure for young children! They are beginning to integrate their oral language skills with written language. To encourage children along the path to early literacy, books must be colorful, engaging, and interesting; they should invite the young reader to explore both the print and the pictures.

People in My Community is a new series designed to help children read about the world around them. In each book young readers will learn interesting facts about some familiar community helpers.

Each book is specially designed to support the young reader in the reading process. The familiar topics are appealing to young children and invite them to read — and re-read — again and again. The full-color photographs and enhanced text further support the student during the reading process.

In addition to serving as wonderful picture books in schools, libraries, homes, and other places where children learn to love reading, these books are specifically intended to be read within an instructional guided reading group. This small group setting allows beginning readers to work with a fluent adult model as they make meaning from the text. After children develop fluency with the text and content, the book can be read independently. Children and adults alike will find these books supportive, engaging, and fun!

— Susan Nations, M.Ed., author, literacy coach, and consultant in literacy development

The doctor has an important job. The doctor helps people stay healthy.

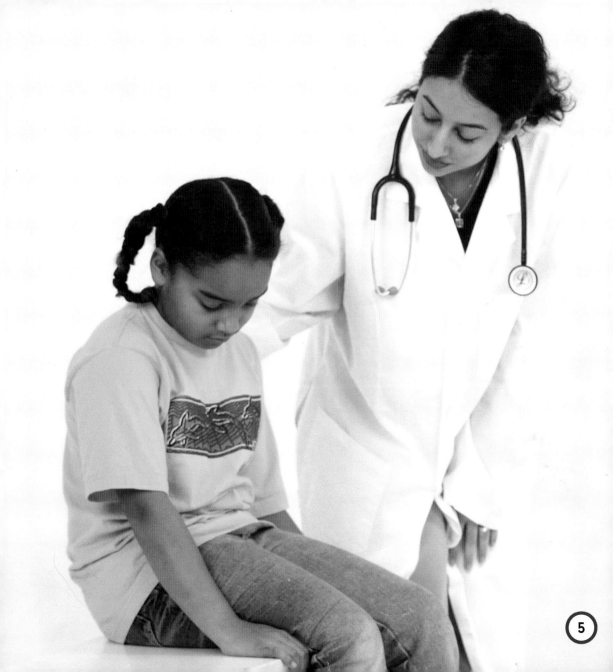

Some doctors
work in hospitals.
Some doctors
work in offices
or clinics.

You should visit the doctor once a year for a checkup to see if you are growing the right way.

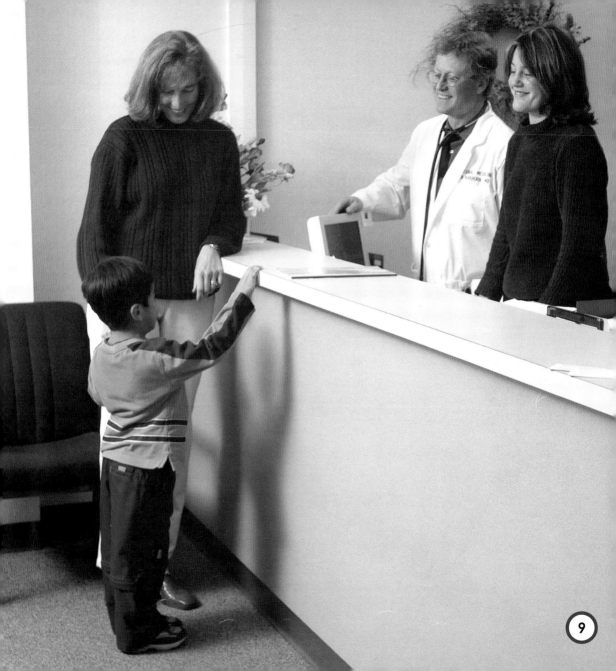

When you visit the doctor, your temperature is taken with a **thermometer**. You get weighed and measured.

thermometer

The doctor checks to see if your heart is healthy. He listens to your heart with a **stethoscope**.

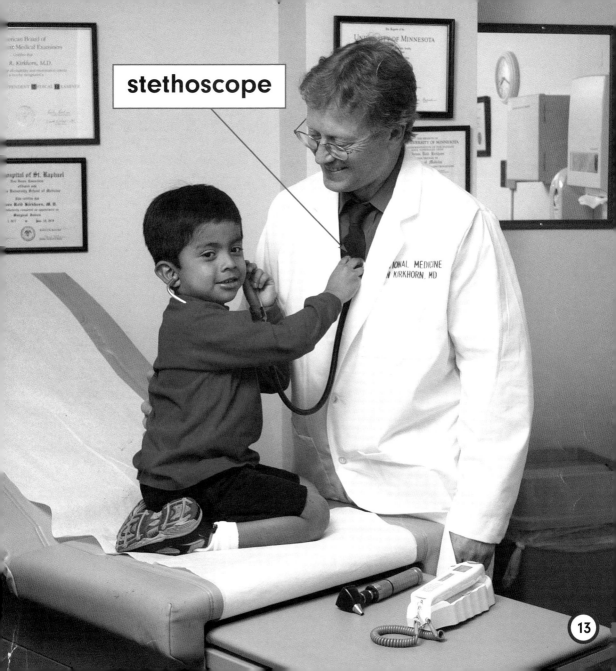

stethoscope

13

The doctor checks inside your ears, nose, and throat with an **otoscope**. Sometimes this tickles!

otoscope

Sometimes the doctor gives you a shot. This might hurt a little, but it helps you stay healthy.

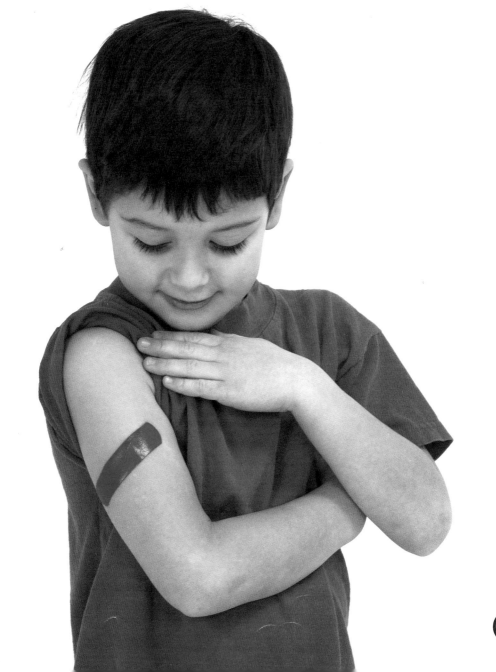

Sometimes it's scary to visit the doctor, but the doctor is nice. He tells you how to stay healthy.

It looks like fun
to be a doctor.
Would you like
to be a doctor
some day?

Glossary

checkup — an examination to see if someone is healthy

clinics — places people go to see doctors

hospitals — places people go when they are hurt or very sick

otoscope — a tool with a light that doctors use to see inside your ears, nose, and throat

For More Information

Fiction Books

Berenstain, Stan and Jan. *The Berenstain Bears Go to the Doctor.* New York: Random House, 1981.

Davison, Martine. *Robby Visits the Doctor.* New York: Random House, 1992.

Gold, Becky. *Phil and Lil Go to the Doctor.* New York: Scholastic, 2001.

Nonfiction Books

Kottke, Jan. *A Day with a Doctor.* New York: Children's Press, 2000.

Moses, Amy. *Doctors Help People.* Plymouth, Minn.: Child's World, 1997.

Web Sites
Going to the Doctor
www.kidshealth.org/kid/feel_better/people/going_to_dr.html
What happens at the doctor's office

Index

About the Author

Jacqueline Laks Gorman is a writer and editor. She grew up in New York City and began her career working on encyclopedias and other reference books. Since then, she has worked on many different kinds of books. She lives with her husband and children, Colin and Caitlin, in DeKalb, Illinois.